WILD CATS!
OF THE WORLD

TIGERS

By Melissa Cole
Photographs by Tom and Pat Leeson

BLACKBIRCH PRESS

GALE GROUP
™
THOMSON LEARNING

Detroit • New York • San Diego • San Francisco
Boston • New Haven, Conn. • Waterville, Maine
London • Munich

Published by Blackbirch Press
10911 Technology Place
San Diego, CA 92127

e-mail: customerservice@galegroup.com
Web site: www.galegroup.com/blackbirch

©2002 by Blackbirch Press
an imprint of the Gale Group
First Edition

Printed in China

10 9 8 7 6 5 4 3 2 1

Library of Congress Cataloging-in-Publication Data
Cole, Melissa
Tigers / by Melissa Cole.
     p.   cm. — (Wild cats of the world)
Summary: Describes the physical characteristics, behavior, habitat, and endangered status of tigers.
    ISBN 1-56711-446-6 (hardcover : alk. paper)
    1. Tigers—Juvenile literature. [1.Tigers. 2. Endangered species.]
    I. Title. II. Series.
QL737.C23 C64 2002
599.75'9—dc21   2001004192

Contents

Introduction

Tigers are the largest members of the cat family. People have long admired their enormous power and graceful beauty. At one time, tigers were found in eastern Russia, China, Southeast Asia, India, and Pakistan, as well as the Caspian Sea region and a large chain of islands in Indonesia. Today, however, they are found in fewer areas of the world. Scientists estimate that more than 100,000 tigers etimated worldwide 100 years ago. Today, scientists say, only about 4,000 to 6,000 tigers remain in the wild.

Left: Today, only about 6,000 tigers remain in the wild.
Opposite: Tigers are the largest members of the cat family.

Members of the Family

Tigers can be divided into different groups depending upon where they live and their heredity. All tigers are basically forest animals. They inhabit all types of woodlands, from wet forests in India to open forests in Indochina. Siberian tigers live in cold, uninhabited mountain forests where the temperature can drop below –28 degrees F. in winter. Bengal tigers endure temperatures reaching well over 100 degrees F.

Siberian tigers live in cold, unihabited mountain forests.

Eight types of tigers lived across Asia before 1900. Three—the Bali, Javan, and Caspian tigers—are now extinct. Five species remain.

Siberian Tiger

Also known as the Amur, Korean, or Manchurian tiger, the Siberian tiger is the largest of all cats. It can weigh up to 800 pounds (363 kg) and can grow as long as 13 feet (4 m) from nose to tail. Only about 200 of these endangered cats are thought to survive in the wild. About 800 Siberian tigers live in captivity.

The Siberian tiger has a pale coat with chocolate brown stripes. In winter, the Siberian tiger's fur grows thick and shaggy. Its nose area, or muzzle, is broader than that of other tigers. The male is larger than the female, and often grows white fur around its neck, like a lion's mane.

Siberian tigers can weigh 800 pounds.

Bengal Tiger

The Bengal tiger, also called the Indian tiger, may reach the same lengths as a Siberian tiger, but its body is smaller and its short fur varies from light yellow to reddish orange with black stripes. The average male Bengal tiger measures 10 feet (3 m) from nose to tail—as long as a full-grown horse!

A Bengal tiger has a smaller body and shorter fur than a Siberian tiger.

There are more Bengal tigers than any other type of tiger. Scientists estimate that 3,000 to 4,000 Bengal tigers now remain in the wild.

South China Tiger

The South China tiger has been found in both the forests and rocky mountain areas of southern China. Today, this tiger is found mainly in the mountainous region of Hunan Province. The South China tiger is slightly smaller than the Bengal, and has fewer, broader stripes. Traditional Chinese practices use tiger bones and body parts in religious ceremonies and medicines. These practices have led to a serious decline in the population of South China tigers. Researchers estimate that only 20 to 30 South China tigers remain in the wild.

Indo-Chinese Tiger

The Indo-Chinese, or Malayan, tiger lives in the dense jungles of Malaysia, Thailand, Burma, and parts of southern Asia. It is smaller than most other types of tigers, with dark, short, narrow stripes. The Indo-Chinese tiger has not been studied as closely as other species. Scientists believe there may be between 1,000 and 1,700 Indo-Chinese tigers left in the wild.

Sumatran Tiger

The Sumatran tiger is found only on the Indonesian island of Sumatra. It is the smallest of the world's remaining tigers, averaging 8 feet (2.4 m)

in length. Sumatran tigers are much darker than other types of tigers. They have more red in their coats and broad black stripes. Poaching—illegally hunting— on Sumatra is widespread. Scientists estimate that fewer than 1,000 Sumatran tigers remain in the wild.

The Sumatran tiger is the smallest of the world's remaining tigers.

The Body of a Tiger

A tiger's body is sleek, strong, and graceful. In a zoo, a tiger's tawny color and bold stripes may make it stand out. In the wild, however, the dark stripes break up the tiger's shape and help it blend with reeds, tall grasses, or stripes of light in the forest.

Tigers are powerful enough to knock down animals more than twice their own weight. They are fast, too. Running at full speed, tigers can clear 13 feet (4 m) in a bound and can leap more than 23 feet (7.4 m).

Much of a tiger's body weight consists of muscle. These muscles lie in thick ropes and bands all over the animal's body. Tigers are strong enough to attack rhinos, steal carcasses from crocodiles, and drag prey twice their size more than a third of a mile!

Like most cats, tigers have retractable claws (that move in and out). They are hidden when the tiger walks so that they stay sharp. Hunting tigers use their claws to wound prey with a quick slash. Claws also grip an animal so that it can't escape.

Tigers use their long canine teeth to stab and kill prey.

A tiger's sharp canine teeth are used for stabbing its prey.

Running at full speed, a tiger can leap more than 23 feet (7.4 m).

Scissor-like molars behind the canines act like knife blades. Tigers have tiny incisors in the front of their mouths that are used to pluck feathers and fur.

A tiger's tongue is covered with tiny hook-like projections. While a house cat's lick might feel like rough sandpaper, a tiger's can actually remove skin! These raspy tongues are used to strip hair and hide from a dead animal. They can even scrape meat from bones.

A tiger's tail, which is often as long as its body, is used for balance when it chases and pounces on prey.

Special Features

Tigers have large eyes and powerful vision. A tiger's night vision is six times better than a human's. Tigers have a special mirror-like membrane at the back of their eyes that reflects extra light in the dark. The same type of membrane appears in house cats—you can see it when their eyes take on a greenish glow in certain light.

Special membranes in a tiger's eyes reflect light in darkness.

A tiger's whiskers allow it to feel nearby objects.

A tiger's whiskers are highly sensitive. These thick hairs grow from the upper lips, cheeks, chin, over the eyes, and on the inside of the foreleg. They allow a tiger to feel nearby objects as it silently stalks its prey.

Like other cats, tigers have excellent hearing. Their ears rotate to listen for the faintest sounds made by potential prey. Female tigers have white spots on the back of their ears to make it easier for cubs to follow their mothers through dense forests.

Scent is important to cats as well. Tigers use their noses to find food and mates and to avoid enemies such as humans.

Social Life

All types of tigers have certain behaviors in common. Most tigers are solitary—they live alone. The main social bond occurs between a mother and her young. Males and females only form pairs temporarily to mate.

Young tigers often roam as nomads for several years before they can take control of a territory. A male tiger's territory will overlap the territories of one or more females depending upon his size and strength.

In areas such as India and Nepal, where there is abundant prey, a male's territory might be anywhere from 20 to 385 square miles (32 to 620 km) in size. In Siberia, where the climate is harsh and food is scarce, a male's range may be from 200 to 1,500 square miles in size (322 to 2,414 km).

Tigers spend most of their lives alone.

Tigers communicate by vocalizing—that is roaring, hissing, and growling. They also use body language as well as scents or chemical signals. Males mark their territory by spraying urine at nose level on trees, shrubs, and tufts of grass along the edges of the area. Females often spray urine when they are ready to mate.

Tigers also have many scent glands. These glands are located around the mouth, cheeks, chin, between the toes, and at the base of the tail. Tigers can leave a scent trail wherever they lie down, when they walk, scratch a tree trunk, or scrape the ground with their hind feet. Such scent marks are like a message on an answering machine. Other animals can tell who left the mark, what their message was, and how long ago they left it!

Tigers also have a special organ on the roof of the mouth that is used to "taste-smell." When a tiger opens its mouth and wrinkles its nose, it tastes the air like a snake does when it flicks its tongue.

Tigers leave scent and scratch marks around the borders of their territory.

Expert Hunters

Tigers are among the most powerful predators on Earth. They are able to ambush their prey from as far as 30 feet (9.1 m) away. Their paws have soft, sensitive pads that allow them to slip through the jungle without making a sound.

A Bengal tiger moves in for a kill.

Tigers can charge from the side or spring from behind to deliver a swift, lethal bite to the back of the neck or the throat. Tigers can eat up to 60 pounds (27.2 kg) of meat in a night.

A tiger will usually hunt big animals that will keep it fed for several days. Siberian tigers hunt moose, elk, deer, and wild boar. Bengal tigers will take on baby elephants, rhinos, deer, gaur (wild cows), water buffalo, and wild pigs. After subduing large prey, tigers usually drag it to a quiet place where they continue to feed on it for several days. When a tiger is hungry, it also hunts small mammals, ground birds, frogs, and fish.

During the day, a tiger spends much of its time sleeping or soaking in a stream or watering hole. Once dusk arrives, it watches for prey that comes to the water to drink. A tiger has to be extremely quiet. If even one animal senses the cat's presence, the animal sends out an alarm call, scaring off all prey within earshot. A tiger fails on at least 9 of every 10 hunting attempts.

Deer are a favorite prey of tigers.

The Mating Game

A male tiger may share his territory with many females, depending upon his size and strength. A female tiger, or tigress, is allowed in a male's territory because he knows that eventually she will provide him with an opportunity to mate.

Tigers breed throughout the year, but most mating occurs from November through April. When a female is ready to mate she becomes restless and noisy. Her noises tell males that she is ready to find a mating partner. She will also leave urine scent marks on surrounding shrubs and trees. Male tigers coming across such marks will pursue the female.

Female tigers may mate with more than one male. Males will compete against one another for her attention. The largest, strongest male usually wins these battles and the loser retreats.

Males often fight to gain a female's attention.

A male and female will remain together for several days during mating season.

Once a pair is alone, they often circle each other, growling and vocalizing. As they get closer, they gently nudge each other, rubbing bodies and nuzzling faces. Eventually the female lies down and they will mate. This occurs many times over a period of several days. Once this behavior is completed, the male wanders off, leaving the female alone to eventually care for the young.

Raising Young

Female tigers are pregnant for slightly more than three months. During her pregnancy, a female will have found a safe and quiet den in which to give birth.

A female usually gives birth to a litter of two to five cubs, each weighing about 2.5 pounds (1.1 kg). Cubs are born with their eyes closed and are completely helpless for the first two weeks of life. After a few days, the tigress slips away to hunt. She needs to feed herself in order to continue producing milk for her young.

Cubs spend many of their days playing with one another.

Young tigers are especially weak and helpless against predators. Only one out of every two cubs survives to adulthood.

A mother nurses her cubs.

As weeks pass, the cubs continue to grow. Though she still nurses them, a tigress will bring back chunks of meat to the den. When cubs eat more solid food, she will drag back a kill and allows the cubs to feed themselves.

At two to three months, cubs leave the den and begin exploring their surroundings. By six months, the tigers spend most of their time exploring, playing, and wrestling.

Eventually, the tigress lets the cubs join her on hunts. The mother tiger is strict. If a cub makes noise while she is trying to hunt, she will growl or swipe at a cub's tender nose. Hunting lessons go on for more than a year. When cubs are ready to begin hunting, she brings injured prey to them and lets them kill it. Eventually she allows the cubs to do most of the hunting.

At about 18 months, the tigress begins to leave the cubs alone for long periods of time. At first, she returns to make sure they are getting enough to eat. After a while, she does not return at all.

Littermates usually stay together for two to eight weeks. Then, each cub will go off to establish a territory of its own and live life as an adult tiger.

Tigers and Humans

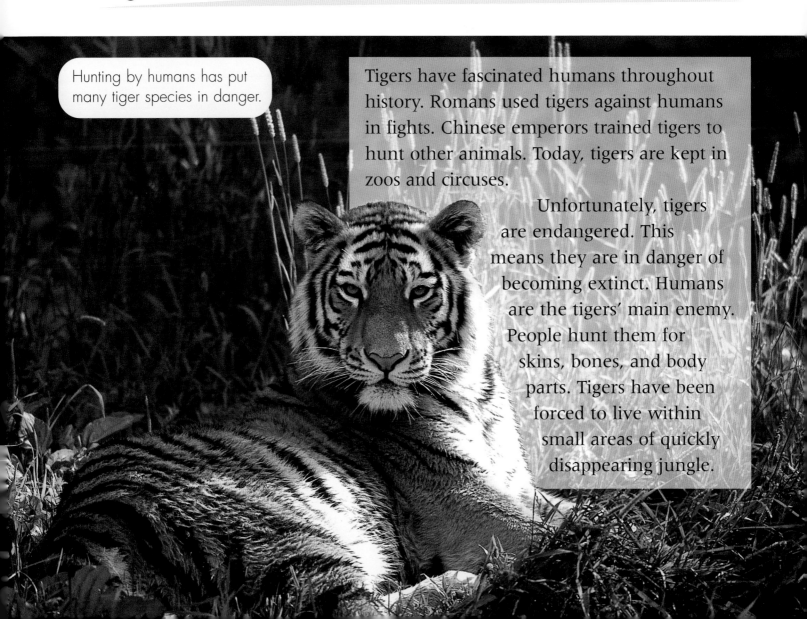

Hunting by humans has put many tiger species in danger.

Tigers have fascinated humans throughout history. Romans used tigers against humans in fights. Chinese emperors trained tigers to hunt other animals. Today, tigers are kept in zoos and circuses.

Unfortunately, tigers are endangered. This means they are in danger of becoming extinct. Humans are the tigers' main enemy. People hunt them for skins, bones, and body parts. Tigers have been forced to live within small areas of quickly disappearing jungle.

For these reasons, tigers and humans are poor neighbors. Tigers have hunted livestock when they don't have enough wild prey. Some old and sick tigers have even attacked and killed humans.

Many people are working hard to save the world's remaining wild tigers. In 1972, India began "Project Tiger," which set aside protected areas where tigers could live. Today, there are 23 Project Tiger preserves. Zoos and aquariums have established breeding programs to raise tigers in captivity. Scientists are constantly trying to learn more about tigers and their needs as well as tracking their current populations. They hope that with enough help, these amazing animals will continue to survive.

Bengal Tiger Facts:

Scientific Name: Panthera tigris tigris
Shoulder Height: 36–38"
Body Length: 9–10 feet from nose to tail
Weight: 395–580 pounds
Color: orange coat with black stripes
Reaches Sexual Maturity: females 3–4 years, males between 4–5 years
Gestation: 3–4 months
Litter Born: 2–4 cubs per litter
Favorite Food: Samba deer, chital deer, water buffalo, wild pigs, guar (wild cows) and monkeys
Range: small populations across India, but most numerous in Bangladesh and west Bengal

Glossary

breed When animals mate and produce young.

extinct When an animal or plant has died out it has become extinct.

heredity The passing of traits from parents to their children.

membrane A very thin layer of tissue on skin that lines certain organs or cells.

poaching Illegally hunting.

prey An animal that is hunted by another animal for food.

tigress A female tiger.

Further Reading

Books

Levine, Stuart P. *The Tiger* (Endangered Animals and Habitats). San Diego, CA: Lucent Books, 1998.

Schafer, Susan. *Tigers* (Animals, Animals). Tarrytown, NY: Benchmark Books, 2000.

Stonehouse, Bernard. *A Visual Introduction to Wild Cats* (Animal Watch). New York: Checkmark Books, 1999.

Thapar, Valmik. *Tiger: Habitats, Life Cycles, Food Chains, Threats* (Natural World). Chatham, NJ: Raintree/Steck Vaughn, 1999.

Web Site

Cyber Tiger—*www.nationalgeographic.com/features/97/tigers/maina.html*

Index